A recommendation from
Charles R. Wood:

I have known Mike for many years, beginning when he first sought help to address his alcohol bondage following a driving conviction in 2007. As we began the therapy process, it soon became evident he had been sent by God to hear a message leading him to greater, personal freedom.

Mike's life story of redemption, restoration, and renewal glorifies God and offers hope to all who feel hopeless.

His story is not finished and, in many aspects, has just begun.

Charles R. Wood

The Answer

the ANSWER

A true life testimonial about anger, depression, addictions, prison, freedom, and salvation

Michael Beeckman

Xulon Press

Xulon Press
2301 Lucien Way #415
Maitland, FL 32751
407.339.4217
www.xulonpress.com

© 2019 by Michael Beeckman

Printed in the United States of America.

ISBN-13: 978-1-5456-7388-1

About the Author

Pastor Michael B. Beeckman is a musician and writer of songs and poetry. He was once serving two life sentences in prison and has now accepted a calling to encourage people to build their faith in God as a witness to the truth. He has been offering testimonials for twenty years now with a group in Saginaw, Michigan called "The Scouts." Their group consists of ex-felons, gang members, drug addicts, drug dealers, prostitutes, victims of rape, and those that have experienced loved ones that have committed suicide. His testimony reflects a brave and bold confession that he offers in an effort to guide people out of depression, anger, resentment, and all of the distractions that inhibit our healthy relationships in life and with God.

This short yet very powerful book is a reflection of the first forty-four years of his life.

Answer / 'ansər/ : a solution of a problem

Table of Contents

Chapter 1
Good ol' American Family

I was born July 18, 1974 in Saginaw, Michigan into a Christian family of four: Dad (Ed), Mom (Colleen), and my younger brother by two and a half years, Jeffry. At that time, phones were attached to the walls and rotary dial was most common because push-button was just invented. The cords were braided at first, and then came the curly cord that stretched so you could move around a little or sit in your favorite chair while sipping coffee. Or, you could talk on the phone while staining the walls yellow with cigarette tar that had been through your lungs and most likely everyone else's in the room, including the baby's. I recall getting a haircut one day and the stylist had a cigarette dangling from the corner of her mouth the entire time. The smoke was forcing her to complete this task with one eye squinted shut, as the side stream smoke that eventually hung onto my hair, rolled up her face, and into her eye.

Plaid, pearl buttons, and big collars were the fashion in the 70s. Polaroid instamatic cameras were new, vinyl records were common, and the 8-track cassette tapes were starting to develop a trend.

As a family, we played board games like Monopoly and Yahtzee. Going out to play really meant Mom and Dad taking us to the park to push us on swings. We were laughing out loud just because our tummies were tickled and it made everyone laugh. Life was definitely different then.

Church was also popular and we attended every Sunday. My parents had me baptized in a Methodist church, even though Mom's side was Protestant and Dad's side was Catholic. The Bible lessons I received there, with awesome stories and crafts that expressed our appreciation for Jesus, still puts a smile on my face because it was learning about peace and joy. My mother especially talked about Him (Jesus) as a shepherd to the Kingdom of Heaven. Her eyes were like a bright, powder blue when she said the name Jesus. "Trust in Him; there is nothing we cannot make it through with Jesus," were words I often heard Mom say. She also taught us that black is beautiful, because God sees us all the same and no one is better than another. The only thing she feared in life was God.

My dad was a very peaceful man and never aggressive; a gentle believer as well. He didn't care much for wrestling with my brother and I because of the chance of someone getting hurt, so Mom would tackle us and take the chance of a fat lip. As I have grown into a man and had children, I am grateful to have an awesome dad! He was never abusive, physically or verbally; neither was Mom. I have met people whose fathers have violated every bit of their being, mothers too, because they also had been violated. My mother disclosed to me that she had been molested as a child. Fortunately, she never took it out on God or any human being for that matter. Mom and Dad tried their best to lead by examples of being God-fearing, Jesus- loving parents.

NOTES:

_____

_____

_____

_____

_____

_____

_____

_____

_____

_____

_____

_____

_____

_____

_____

_____

_____

_____

_____

_____

Chapter 2

God Love

It wasn't just my parents as examples; I will never forget my second-grade teacher, Mrs. Mary Jackson. She was confirmation to Mother's words that black certainly is beautiful! Mrs. Jackson was tall and constantly smiling, unless she had to put my name on the board for being rambunctious. She put other kids' names on too, but I remember mine being more frequent. I was always hyper and struggled with focus, like writing here, birds chirping, and the sump pump sure seems noisy... Back to Mrs. Jackson. However, I recently had the honor of telling her she is one of the reasons I know God exists. The look on her face when I made my way over to her table at a church function was priceless. I'm a bald, white guy with a white beard now and blue eyes. "Who's this man walking up to me?" she said, after I told her she looked no different than she did in 1981; this was 2018. That Jesus joy shined from her eyes toward all of her students. I learned not only grammar and arithmetic in her classroom, but that Jesus's love comes in all races. We are one race in the eyes of God.

NOTES:

_____

_____

_____

_____

_____

_____

_____

_____

_____

_____

_____

_____

_____

_____

_____

_____

_____

_____

_____

_____

Chapter 3
The Divorce and Abandonment

While no one is perfect, Mom and Dad fell out of love and into separation, divorcing when I was eight. At the time, Dad was working for General Motors and was constantly being laid off. So he pursued a greater education to later become an electrical engineer; a position that moved him to Ohio where he remarried. My brother and I felt abandoned, and the every-other-weekend visits from dad ceased. He did a lot of fun things during his time with us: trips with the family to go camping or just the three of us to Cedar Point or Kentucky where my aunt and uncle lived with more cousins. So when he moved, all those activities were no longer practical.

We felt so torn and displaced. Something was missing, because a part of us was gone. Mom cried a lot, but she seemed to calm down as the three of us would hug it out. Love has that effect on people. She would find babysitters for us as she worked and also searched for a companion. We understood and most of the sitters became like older sisters to us, because Mom wasn't having someone take care of us that didn't love kids.

NOTES:

_____

_____

_____

_____

_____

_____

_____

_____

_____

_____

_____

_____

_____

_____

_____

_____

_____

_____

_____

Chapter 4

New Family

Mom met this wonderful Catholic man, Ray, with four daughters and two sons. He was so genuine and made sure he acknowledged Jeff and I. He would even tuck us in at night. One night, Jeff and I told Mom to leave the room, as we had to discuss something with Ray. We asked him if he would marry our mom. This man loved our mother and it showed, so they married very soon after. So we moved in with all of them, eight of us at the time: three bedrooms, one bathroom. They lived in poverty, yet it did not seem to faze them. The culture was a bit shocking to Jeff and I, but we quickly adjusted. Everyone got one pair of shoes a year, school shoes, unless we stole them or found a less-used pair in the shoe store dumpster.

Ray was a Catechism teacher at St. Andrews where we attended as a family. I loved Catechism, but napped during Sunday services. Commencement, confirmation, and communion classes were a lot of fun and the lessons will sustain in my heart forever. Catholic practices have always been powerful, but too quiet and routine for me. I truly never felt like the sacraments were the way to know Jesus. The motions were just something we needed to go through; it seemed like it ought to be much more simple.

Ray was also chairman of the Moose lodge where "The Parents," as my siblings and I called them, spent a lot of time. They were drinkers and often drank more than they could handle. Arguments would result in overnight stays at Grandma's house. We would return home the next day after a sober reconciliation between them.

My older step-brother, who was the oldest sibling still living at home, was in high school and also our overseer on many occasions. He was at that age where partying with drugs, sex, and rock & roll were as cool as cool could get. Most of the neighborhood kids hung out at our house because our parents were seldom home and opportunities for real fun were abundant.

We were forced to fight each other; if you refused, you would pay a consequence greater than losing. These were called "Friendship Fights," and afterward, you had to be "friends," as that was the only rule. We learned how to throw a punch and take a punch. For me, it was that one strike that would put me in a fiery hail of kicks and throws. I didn't want to but was all or nothing. Most of the others were anxious for their round; the older ones that made us fight placed bets.

Neighborhood mothers would pound on our door, demanding an explanation as to why their kid's glasses were broken or their eye was swollen. "We were playing and he fell," seemed to be an answer frequently given at our front door. Boys will be boys. I need to get a patent on an idea for a "Lame Excuse" rolodex, as we sure came up with some really good ones. Then again, that's just lying; not something I want to prosper from. Games were invented in our house as darkness fell. If you chose not to participate, again there were consequences. And never, ever nark (snitch). Sorry, there are some things I cannot disclose for the sake of others from Step #9 in AA - *Made direct amends except when to do so may injure others.* This truly does make sense. If you need to ask for forgiveness, you should and always grant forgiveness if you want to be forgiven. This reminds me of a Scripture that has truly guided me to spiritual freedom:.

Matthew 6:14 ~ *For if you forgive men their trespasses, your heavenly Father will also forgive you, 15 But if you do not forgive men their trespasses, neither will your Father forgive your trespasses*

NOTES:

_____

_____

_____

_____

_____

_____

_____

_____

_____

_____

_____

_____

_____

_____

_____

_____

_____

_____

_____

_____

Chapter 5

A Boy Hits Puberty

As I entered into middle school and puberty, I began to make friends, lots of them. Guitar became a huge interest also. Two of my cousins, Bob and Greg, were so cool, because they always led the family with guitars and piano during the holidays. One of my friends let me borrow his guitar until his parents asked for it back. Finally, my dad ended up taking me to *Watermelon Sugar* on Hamilton Street in Old Town Saginaw with my cousin Greg to buy my first guitar for my thirteenth birthday! This was also an effort on his part to keep me occupied. Learning my favorite riffs and cranking the amp toward the open window became my practice for attention. This thing came very natural to me though. All I wanted to do was learn and practice. When friends came over, they would ask me to play and I began to make friends that were also learning to play guitar.

I also got into a lot of fights in school and out of school. Again, I hated fighting but it loved me, leading to suspensions and poor grades. I really could not have cared less about grades then.

We spent a great deal of time stealing bikes, booze, and whatever someone else had worked hard for. Then, one day someone stole my bike. What was even worse, I was still on the bike. Some long-haired guy twice as big as me, and with twice my temper, yanked me off and smiled all while stealing my bike. I knew it was best to lose the bike and not an eye as well, a "no win" situation here. This just made me more angry about life for another reason. I gave up stealing bikes, as I learned about karma from it.

Vandalism seemed appealing now. We even broke into a few homes and stole guns to sell or just carry, as if we were gangsters. I was one of the few white kids in our little clique. For some reason, I just wanted to be a thug. This lifestyle got me jumped more than once by the same darn group; I mean, stomped too. One of them, a mexican dude that hated blonde-headed white boys, took advantage of me being alone behind a house at a party with one of his black homies. They jumped on me till I hit the ground, then put Fila shoe prints on my forehead. Another time I was on the east side, walking with a buddy who asked me to go along so he wouldn't be alone on the way home . It was nighttime and the same group came out from between two houses. One got on down behind me while the other swung at my face. So I fell over the guy as they'd planned and, again, ended up with Fila shoe prints on my face, probably the same pair of shoes too. This did not deter me from consequences or my choice of lifestyle.

At one time, three of us (Mike, Mike, and Chuck) had just broken into a cop's house and stolen his gun collection and ammo. I honestly remember he conveniently left his gun safe unlocked when we got to it. As we sat in my friend's basement, we were examining and handling the weapons. I recall smoking weed once we got to the hangout. Beastie Boys "Licensed to Ill" was blasting on a dual cassette jam box. This was around 1987; I would have been thirteen. Then "BOOM!" The .357 revolver exploded as my boy pulled the trigger to test the hammer action. See, they were talking about one semi-automatic pistol, as I was loading that one to see the difference in the weight with bullets in it. The couch we were on was facing a concrete wall. My ears are still ringing over thirty years later after firing that gun.

Coincidentally, all three of us would later be serving life in prison at the same time but on different cases, all murder convictions. They were on a case and tried together. The two of them robbed a drug house with four people in it. They tied everyone up, executed them, and then burned the house down. About five years ago, Mike escaped from a medium security prison. They caught up to him in less than 24 hours and locked him into super-max, where he most likely is now.

I was so full of anger and testosterone. I tried diluting it all with alcohol and other substances. I had lost my virginity at fourteen and lied about my age to get invited to the more adult parties. I met one of my best friends in a substance abuse class. By then, I'd been arrested twice for shoplifting and lied about where I was going or had been, even though Mom always seemed to know exactly where those places were and who I was with. She did everything she could, including counseling with therapists and allowing me to be detained in jail for different reasons.

NOTES:

_____

_____

_____

_____

_____

_____

_____

_____

_____

_____

_____

_____

_____

_____

_____

_____

_____

_____

_____

Chapter 6

Change is Good

At fifteen, my mom had enough of my delinquency, so she asked my dad if he would take me. Moving to Ohio would give Dad and I a chance to bond and a fresh start for me to pick new friends. This worked, as my grades even shot up to a 3.8 GPA. I had met some terrific new friends, joined the weightlifting team, and played football. Popularity came, but so did the attraction to sex and drugs. Satan found a way to influence me again.

> **Isaiah 14:12** KJV ~ *"How you are fallen from heaven, O Lucifer, son of the morning! How you are cut down to the ground, You who weakened the nations!"*

I had once again found my way into a careless, alcoholic lifestyle.

We were going to church every Sunday, Methodist and then Pentecostal. This "Living Word" church really was alive. It was the first time I ever saw someone fall out in service. This giant black dude went down and cleared like three rows of metal folding chairs when he hit. The next week, they had ushers or deacons behind people, prepared to catch them and lay them down nice and easy. But this effort by my dad and stepmother was truly all they could do to try and save me.

NOTES:

_____

_____

_____

_____

_____

_____

_____

_____

_____

_____

_____

_____

_____

_____

_____

_____

_____

_____

Chapter 7

Caving In

There were so many things that were important to me: attention, getting high, making friends to have more people in a party, things that were distracting me from God and His plans. Back then, cell phones and internet were just being developed. Thank God, or I may have never had time to practice guitar. Porn would have been at my fingertips everywhere I went, not just in a magazine hidden underneath the bottom of my dresser that I had to pull out completely to get to where that and my stash always was.

At the age of sixteen, my dad had enough of my delinquency and our relationship was out of order. All of my acting out, lying about where I was going, and sneaking out of the house brought things to a close. One night, as I was sneaking back into the house, I knocked over a series of metal TV tables Dad had butted up against the front and back doors so he would know when I got home. He came out with a flashlight and shined it in my face as I lay in bed. The beam of light hit the underside of my chin, where it had been split open by a fist at a party I'd just left. Disciplinary action had to be taken and I hated discipline.

NOTES:

_____

_____

_____

_____

_____

_____

_____

_____

_____

_____

_____

_____

_____

_____

_____

_____

_____

_____

Chapter 8

The Warning

By this time my dad and stepmom had filed unruly charges against me, put me on probation, and had me detained in juvenile jail for insubordination and drug use after several attempts with counseling. So I demanded I go back to live with my mom in Michigan. Finally he and mom caved in and reluctantly allowed me to return to Saginaw.

The last supper we shared in Ohio was the most memorable. I'll never forget the moment my father looked at me; his eyes were filled with hurt and desperation but also love still. The Holy Spirit spoke through him. He said, "Son, if you move back to Saginaw, within six months you will be spending the rest of your life in prison." God does speak through us in His efforts to connect and deliver messages, much like the prophets of the Bible. Those words went straight to my heart and since it was already in dismay, they added fuel to the fire. By the time we reached the exit into Saginaw, I had thought only of who I was going to contact to get drunk with and if they weren't around, who I would look for next. I was never thinking of Mom's feelings, or anyone else's for that matter; just mine. Dad dropped me off and pulled away without either of us saying goodbye. It was dark out and darkness had certainly fallen.

NOTES:

_____

_____

_____

_____

_____

_____

_____

_____

_____

_____

_____

_____

_____

_____

_____

_____

_____

_____

_____

_____

Chapter 9

Evil is Real

Shortly thereafter, I was in an old apartment building that was once a hotel and brothel in the late 1800s and early 1900s: The Ippel's building, on the same block that the Fordney Hotel existed. This place stunk of human urine, body odor, crack, weed, stale beer, liquor, and whatever else that had stained these walls for more than a century. The hallways were poorly lit, so dark it was hard to tell what color of paint was on the walls. Decades of foot traffic made a worn path in the center of the hallway floor. You could hear noises from the multitude of rooms that prostitutes, pimps, and drug dealers could rent by the day, week, or month. Whatever you needed, this place had it, especially evil.

I recall this one night there very clearly. I had not been drinking or high on anything, and we had no luck scoring so I decided to head home. In the apartment I was in were two females and one other guy. I walked out the door and when I pulled the door shut behind me, it was as if I stepped into a vacuum. My ears must have popped or something. The evident on-goings in the other apartments were missing, and this was on the second or third floor. The stairs to the exit were now only lit by the light from a lamppost, reflecting off the sidewalk and through the window. Then it fell upon me: Evil; Heavy-weight, huge, cold, and overbearing. It was like you see a vampire wrap his cape around its victim, except I could not see anything but knew I couldn't breath and the sense of a demonic presence was certain. Chills and adrenaline hit me like never before. It took everything I had to break through and rush back up to the apartment and pound on the door. Terror was on my face when they opened the door, so much so that when the two girls looked at me, they started to scream. My buddy grabbed a baseball bat and I slammed the door shut. He had no idea. I shouted, "There is something out there! Do not walk out that door. I couldn't see it but felt it!" This put the girls into hysterics. Whatever was in my eyes and on my face was confirmation that this wasn't a prank. After we had an opportunity to calm down and get a grip, we opened the door together. Life was back to normal in the old Ippel's hotel: the smell, the sounds, the history. Somehow I felt like I was being mocked the entire walk home that night.

Old town Saginaw has been known for hauntings and demonic experiences. Its history reflects this, while movies have been made down there for that appeal. Interesting documentaries some may have taken lightly as entertainment, but I suggest people do not gamble with this area, hoping to capture anything on video. I warn you; what gets captured may not be camera footage but someone's soul.

Selfish behavior, recklessness, and self-destruction were all I focused on at that time. I sold my guitar for drugs and liquor. Priorities. Sex, drugs, and heavy metal that carried messages about having no remorse and no regrets were all that fed my poor self-esteem. One night, I even did the act of "blood brothers" at a party. The pony keg was only a foot away when I took the stiletto switchblade across the palm of my left hand. Alcohol really does thin the blood. As I pulled the blade across, the blood just sprayed and I can't forget the piercing scream of some female that was standing close enough for the blood to land on her jacket. I lied at the hospital. We couldn't tell them where the party house was, so I said some guy tried to rob us at a football game. It made me sound tougher too. On a different night, I wound up involved in a huge brawl and took two hits from a hockey stick. The first one literally knocked me out of a shoe. The second went across my back, as I scrambled to avoid one in the head. Good Lord... This was that "Downward spiral" the psychiatrists all concurred on.

NOTES:

_____

_____

_____

_____

_____

_____

_____

_____

_____

_____

_____

_____

_____

_____

_____

_____

_____

_____

_____

_____

_____

Chapter 10

Satan Wants Us Dead

by Pastor Michael Beeckman

Satan needs no rest, so he never sleeps.
He wants us all depressed, to the point we cannot eat.
He wants to bring us pain, as if it never stops,
To make us blame our woes directly onto God.
Satan watched and laughed as Christ was crucified.
After three short days, we find our Saviour is alive.
And so the devil saw, but continues to conspire
Ways to bring us doubt, for Satan is a liar!

Satan wants us dead; doesn't care how long it takes.
So let man lie with man, a child they'll never make.
He leads the race of hate, killing those God loves,
Desperate to destroy faith, hope, and love.
He knows what turns us on, leading us to sin.
Drink until we're drunk, distracting us within.
His ways will make you feel, "There must not be a God."
The reason he's in hell is he could not be on top.

The Father, Son, and Spirit want us all to live
But Satan hates our Lord and everything He gives,
Planting seeds of hate, growing crops of death;
Blooms of evil waste, harvesting the end.
So Jesus brought us hope; He proved the devil wrong.
Our Saviour set us free from the evil one.
Listen to the Word, its pages must be read.
Within, we find the warnings — Satan wants us dead.

NOTES:

_____

_____

_____

_____

_____

_____

_____

_____

_____

_____

_____

_____

_____

_____

_____

_____

_____

_____

_____

_____

Chapter 11

Confirmation in Dad's Warning

Still sixteen, less than six months from the time my father delivered a warning, I was with some friends in an apartment we had broken into; the apartment was directly next door from my house. It stood as a central party location to where we all lived at the time. We knew the tenant wasn't going to be home for the night and this was one of our gathering places. It was the middle of winter in Michigan, so outdoor partying wasn't an option. Our plan was only to enter through an unlocked window, party, and pick up before we leave so there would be no evidence we'd been there. The other tenants in this old building were used to the sounds coming from this particular apartment so we had no worries. As we engaged in drinking, we became heavily intoxicated. Drunken wrestling was something we often did and one of the guys had been rummaging through the tenant's belongings. He found a couple of shotgun shells and cut them open. With a lighter, he was igniting little piles of powder in an ashtray, creating little mushroom clouds in the kitchen. This was so cool that I decided to raise the bar a little and took a can of spray deodorant with a lighter in front of it to create a blowtorch to light the little piles. Then I turned the flame on to my friend's butts. This was funny for a moment. Then I lit the back of the couch on fire. The oldest of us four sobered enough to say, "Let's call it a night, guys."

We attempted to extinguish the flames by smacking it with our hands. As the three of them walked out ahead of me, I gave the couch one last, little blast. We got several blocks up and one of the guys suggested we make sure the fire was out. Well, by the time we returned, that apartment was engulfed in flames. In winter months, homes become extremely dry and dangerously vulnerable. The couch sat next to the exit where just outside was the stairway that led to the upstairs apartments; this was also the only exit. While some were sleeping upstairs, their rooms filled with smoke. We truly made efforts to wake them and eventually caught a couple of children their father tossed down to us from a second-story window. Time never reverses. History may seem to repeat itself, but you cannot undo an action like a cursor on a computer will. Two people died that night; a pregnant mother and her young daughter. For every action, there is always a reaction.

The following morning, police and investigators were doing a canvas of the neighborhood while a team was trying to determine the origin of the fire. News teams were covering the incident and we actually accepted an interview that made us look like heroes.

People thanked us for our courage and we even watched it on the six o'clock broadcast.

As the investigation went on, they had determined arson was the cause and it turned into a homicide case as well. Everything in the building was not completely destroyed. One of our members had actually stolen some items, including a jacket that would later prove us at the scene of the crime, leading to a simultaneous search of four homes six days later. Ours was one of them. As the police squad woke us all up at two am, they made us sit at our dining room table. My mom was hyperventilating while my stepdad was glaring at me, as if he wanted to choke me. I confessed and they arrested me on open murder and arson.

Since I was only sixteen, they locked me up in the Saginaw County Juvenile Detention Center. With a court- appointed attorney, the prosecutor decided they would try me on first-degree murder. The law states that when someone has committed a felony and somebody dies as a result, it is in fact murder, regardless of an intent to kill. So we took it to trial in an effort to fight the case, since I honestly had no premeditation in this. A jury was selected and the trial began. During the trial, I would be made to look like a heartless murderer. The prosecutor made efforts to make me out to be racist, as the two that died were Laotian. A remark had been made by an acquaintance to console me at one point before my arrest, saying, "They didn't even speak English." When this came up in trial, this particular witness that the prosecutor had called for this statement made him look dirty. His witness denied ever even telling him I was the one that said it. The truth presented itself. I was offered a lesser charge as a plea bargain, but my lawyer advised us to let the jury decide my fate.

After a two-week trial, the jury was hopelessly deadlocked. A mistrial was ordered and because I had taken the stand to testify, retrial was the next motion. It would not be dismissed. The prosecutor again offered a plea agreement of second-degree murder, with no guarantee of sentencing parameters. At this point, my attorney convinced us to accept the offer, since it would guarantee a second chance at freedom. He used this to talk us into accepting the plea agreement. A conviction of first degree carries a mandatory life sentence without the possibility of parole.

After pleading guilty to second-degree murder, a lengthy process to determine sentencing took place. I was transported for psychological evaluations, while still being held in the juvenile detention center. The judge had the option of sentencing me as an adult or juvenile. After 410 days from the day I was arrested, the judge sentenced me. I received two life sentences in prison, one for each murder conviction, with ten to twenty years for the arson charge. What our attorney told us apparently was not a fact. Life just got REAL. We immediately filed for an appeal on the sentence with the Michigan Supreme Court.

Police say fire set to hide jacket theft

Pair face charges in two deaths

BY BOB SOLT
and THOMAS NORD
News Staff Writers

(991)

The theft of a Detroit Pistons jacket may have sparked a Feb. 1 fire that killed a Saginaw mother and her daughter, a court document indicates.

In an affidavit filed for a warrant to search a house at ▮ N. Fayette, Saginaw Police Detective ▮▮▮▮ said his probe determined the fire was set to conceal the theft of the jacket, a wristwatch and a flashlight from the downstairs apartment where the blaze apparently started.

Police found the missing items at ▮ N. Fayette, the home of 17-year-old ▮▮▮▮▮▮ at the time of the fire, ▮▮▮▮▮▮▮▮▮▮▮ Assistant Prosecutor Howard Gave said today.

According to the affidavit, Dolson also recovered an aerosol spray can believed used in setting the blaze.

The affidavit states that the spray was directed across an open flame, creating a "blow torch" effect.

The can was discovered under an exterior

Michael Beeckman

NOTES:

_____

_____

_____

_____

_____

_____

_____

_____

_____

_____

_____

_____

_____

_____

_____

_____

_____

_____

_____

_____

Chapter 12

Oppression to Depression

Shackles are extremely cold and uncomfortable, painful from the skin to the soul. As I wore them in the inmate transportation van, amongst everyone else headed to Ionia for whatever length of terms they'd been given, for whatever offense they'd been charged, I fought tears. I swallowed them as if I was tough. But I was scared and ashamed on the inside. My heart ached like never before. I felt so terrible for what I'd done. The pain I had caused for families as well as my own made me sick. Remorse was so overwhelming and there was nothing I wanted more than to reverse all of this. But the van kept moving forward. We arrived at our destination, where apparently not all were getting off here. A few were just going to some camp for rehabilitation and an opportunity to start over shortly thereafter. Not me. I was about to be escorted by gunmen, while shackled, into what looked like a medieval castle: cold, loveless, and dark. This was only the first stop: Quarantine. Here is where they classify you and place you accordingly, depending on the number of years you have been given. It was in quarantine that the counselor made it clear that L-I-F-E means forever in this existence of your being. "I do not care what your lawyer led you to believe. You will never be released from prison," said the man.

I went back to my cell and cried. Grievance set in and I became depressed overnight. The next day I had no appetite. A couple of thugs on the yard tried to corner me and called me a "bitch." This is a term that sets your pace as you live here in prison. Well, I started swinging on both of them, as if this white boy was setting a different pace. The entire yard was in an uproar. Guess the white boys usually accept this title of "bitch." Many do, but not all, and certainly not this one. Looking back, I was kind of prepared for this. God allows things to happen not out of enjoyment in watching us suffer, but for the sake of gaining strength for what is ahead. I gained some respect for a few days from others, but the rush wore off and depression set back in again. I snuck a disposable razor back to my cell, where I was going to stomp it to retrieve the blade and cut my wrists after count time to make sure I would have time to bleed out and die. I wanted this over.

NOTES:

Chapter 13

A Spiritual Visit

Now would be the second time in life I would experience the presence of a Spirit. This time it wasn't evil; it was the Holy Spirit! I felt some Jesus love. Hallelujah. He sat down on my bunk next to me. I couldn't see Him but I knew He was there. The sense of love and assurance was so real. I felt Him tell me not to follow through, as there were plans and I should not despair. This feeling brings me to tears now as I write because it was real and true. The next morning, I ditched the razor in a trash can and focused on just doing time and learning how to adapt.

Jeremiah 29:11 ~ *For I know the plans I have for you, says the Lord, plans of peace and not evil, to give you a future and hope.*

NOTES:

Chapter 14

A Place Unlike Home

I was then transferred to another dungeon, Michigan Reformatory. It was also called "Gladiator School." Man, this place was even worse. I walked in carrying my bedding toward my cell block and along the way, some muscle-bound black guy that must've weighed 250 pounds, and could probably have kicked Mike Tyson's title clear, whistled at me, like men at a construction site whistle at women passing by. Yup, at me this time. I looked at him and his group that were all snickering, waiting for my response. I shook my head and pressed on forward. There was a ten-foot fence with concertina razor wire wrapping the top between us, as they were outside on their recreational yard time. For some reason, that wire gave me a sense of security just then.

As I walked into the threshold of what would be home now, I looked up. On the top of the five-story building was a gunman. He was lined right up with the walkway that led into J-Block where I was headed. He had a smirk and, without words, his face said, "Welcome."

Entering the cell block, I could hear all kinds of racket and sounds that were in no rhythm. Men shouting for their cell doors to be open, as if they had any rights or authority. A stretch of showers was at the beginning of each floor that led to a line of cells referred to as "The Rock." For every floor, there were two guards assigned to oversee one hundred-and-twenty inmates. Concrete floors, walls, and ceiling. The cells had three concrete walls and one wall of bars, like a human kennel and much like when you visit an animal shelter and dogs are endlessly barking.

Sad and angry at the same time, I felt the eyes upon me, checking me out and sizing me up. I would be tested again soon thereafter. The Rock was fifty yards long, with windows to the left facing the yard and cells on the right. The yard consisted of sand and gravel, minimal grass with lots of weeds, two basketball courts without nets on the hoops, a worn track for walking or jogging around it all, and some tables strategically positioned so the tower guards with rifles could view everything. "Your house is 61, Beeckman," commanded the officer. I was walking to Cell # 61, passing all kinds of prisoners in their kennels. Don't look directly at anyone; catch a glimpse in your peripheral vision only.

I could hear the motor cranking my cell door open. It was a loud, rackety hum, with a motor, sprockets, and a chain. Concern for insulation as a noise barrier was not an expense the state was going to shell out for luxury. Steel and concrete, while the walls and bars were a "vomit green" and the stainless steel toilet and sink had no welcome mat before it as I stepped into my house. This is where you were to spend 23 hours of each day, with one hour of yard time per day.

NOTES:

_____

_____

_____

_____

_____

_____

_____

_____

_____

_____

_____

_____

_____

_____

_____

_____

_____

_____

_____

Chapter 15

Encouraged by Suicide

Within a week's time, I was walking the yard for my daily exercise. Everyone goes counterclockwise: whites with whites, blacks with blacks, Mexicans with Mexicans. Segregation is an unwritten rule. Stick to your own kind or people make assumptions. I was passing by this table of whites and their leader pulled me over. "Hey man, let me kick it with you a minute." Most of them had their heads shaved and I immediately noticed a pair of lightning bolts tattooed on some of their necks. This guy also had a teardrop inked under his right eye. Shirtless, he had crappy tattoos all over and his eyes were deep and dark brown. Zero emotion. He asked me what I was in for. After I told him, he said, "Who you planning to run with? You might need some protection and we can provide it." They were the Aryan Brotherhood. I looked over his shoulder and noticed this taller dude with longer hair and a ball cap turned backwards. The look on his face was priceless. He was being "protected" alright. I returned the offer with, "I don't need your protection," and I pressed on. I was raised and knew that racism was not part of who I am. There was another white guy on my rock that lived two

47

cells down from me in 63. He wasn't digging the race game either. We called him "Country"; white boy with a Southern accent that preferred to keep to himself much like I was. I don't recall the offense he was in for, but do remember he was only serving 10-20 years for something. One night after count, I had just fallen asleep. Then I heard a shouting, "Assistance at 63, assistance at 63!" Country had hung himself on his bars with his bootlaces. As they cut him down and laid his lifeless body on the rock, prisoners were cheering; they were happy to see a white man dead. They were shaking their cages and yelling, "Thanks for the late night power, Country!" See, after count time, they shut power and lights to all the cells but had to kick the lights on to perform CPR on someone that had been dead at least thirty minutes since the last cell check.

NOTES:

_____

_____

_____

_____

_____

_____

_____

_____

_____

_____

_____

_____

_____

_____

_____

_____

_____

_____

_____

Chapter 16

Consoled by the Spirit

Now came some nausea to fight. Just as I was learning to accept and adapt to this place, the one guy I was making friends with was gone, forever. I couldn't call Mom right now either, as I wasn't sure when my next phone privilege would be. I sat there on my bunk thinking, "He did it. It's over." His time has ended and he didn't have to deal with this for 10-20 years or ever.

A sense of enlightenment came over me. I felt encouraged to join him. I even already had a razor in my cell. Wow, how they would all cheer if two of us died in one night. It would incite a riot. My heart was pounding in my chest. The very second I was about to make up my mind, He sat down next to me once again. It was a messenger of God. "Do not despair. You must consider what He has just put His mother through now." I immediately thought about what my mother would feel if the prison had to deliver this message to her. Ok, God. Thank you.

NOTES:

_____

_____

_____

_____

_____

_____

_____

_____

_____

_____

_____

_____

_____

_____

_____

_____

_____

_____

Chapter 17

Confirmation of the Message

Four-and-a-half years of this prison life had passed. I earned my GED and was reading all sorts of literature. I had become a barber for the inmates and was lifting a lot of weights. I studied music theory and my family members made sure I received subscriptions to as much educational material as they could send. I was also able to practice guitar and become part of the musical program. The prisons had become so over-crowded that the state had to add a bunk to every cell. We all had roommates. Like it or not, you had to share your 8' by 10' cell and toilet with someone else. No more personal space. My bunkie happened to be an old friend from before either of us had been to prison. He was also serving life.

Then the letter came. The Michigan Supreme Court had ordered me to be resentenced to a lesser term of years. "A life sentence should be reserved for offenders with forethought, of which this case does not support." My prayers and my family's prayers were being answered. I was going to get another chance at freedom.

I went back in front of the original sentencing judge, where he reversed my sentence to 10-20 years and applied credit for the time I had served up to this point. I would see the parole board in less than five years. They then reclassified me as a medium security inmate, where I really got into learning and tutoring.

NOTES:

_____

_____

_____

_____

_____

_____

_____

_____

_____

_____

_____

_____

_____

_____

_____

_____

_____

_____

_____

_____

Chapter 18
Preparing for Freedom

I taught a music theory class for a while and also became chairman of Alcoholics Anonymous. They also made it mandatory that I attend group psychotherapy for anger management and impulse control, just like you see on TV with twelve guys sitting in a circle of seats led by a psychiatrist. This time, I was genuinely participating for my benefit in therapy. I also signed up for vocational counseling, a program designed to help inmates learn how to interview and practice etiquette. The behaviours I had learned and practiced for the last eight-and-a-half years were not going to be acceptable or beneficial in the free world.

The time came to see the parole board and they granted my freedom. I was getting that second chance the Lord had assured me of, and was so glad I hadn't gone through with suicide. Once I paroled, my sister-in-law helped me get a job that would sustain me for fifteen years. Thank you, Cassie.

NOTES:

Chapter 19
Giving Back to the Community

I co-founded a group with some friends called, "The Scouts." We would voluntarily go into schools, churches, and colleges to give testimonials about where bad decisions lead us. This was 1999. I personally wanted to bring hope and encourage people, especially youth, to consider consequences. Our goal was also to encourage diversity in the communities. Accept people and love them. We wanted people to see their true potentials. Our group would be in front of small classrooms to full auditoriums, with ten people at times to literally hundreds. Members of our group would include gang members, prostitutes, drug dealers, drug addicts, alcoholics, rape victims, you name it.

Fortunately, I have never really been overly nervous when it came to presentation. Tutoring in prison and taking the position of chairman in AA gave me practice for this.

I started giving music lessons, both private and group classes. This really helped me build relationships in the community. First, I was teaching through one of Saginaw's music stores. Then, I opened up my own studio. I had my own business, and I got busy. My approach was also to be patient and tender-hearted with any students. Every age, race, and gender were coming to see Mr. Mike. I love the feeling of teaching people something they can appreciate that gives them a true sense of confidence; the gift that keeps on giving.

On more than one occasion, one of my students' parents told me I should be a minister or pastor. I laughed it off because well, if they only knew my past. I wasn't worthy of such a title.

NOTES:

Chapter 20

Bad Things Happen to Good People

Life was going along great. I found a woman I'd known since middle school, we fell in love, and we bought a house together. We got married and had a baby girl. She also had a boy from a previous relationship and I assumed the father figure in his life too, as his dad was not in the picture. He had been abandoned. Nonetheless, we were all trying to be a family and make the best of it.

Two days after our daughter was born, my wife and i were still in the hospital recovering from delivery. I received a call from a different hospital. They told me there had been an accident and the family requested my presence.

As I entered the hospital, they escorted me to a private room. The moment I stepped in, I noticed what family members were absent. My brother shot our mother and stepfather in their sleep. Then he sat down in the living room and wrote a letter. It was more of a poem, explaining how dark he felt life was. In it, he made reference to euthanasia as mercy killing. He believed an end was coming for my mom and stepfather and didn't want it to be painful. I feel he didn't want to go alone. He then turned the gun on himself. Jeff had become depressed and was drinking heavily after learning his wife had cheated on him. They all died that day.

I shook my fist at God. "Why would you let something so bad happen to someone so faithful!" The hurting was so deep and I needed understanding now, but it wasn't God's time to explain.

Luke 6:21 ~ *Blessed are you who weep now, For you shall laugh*

NOTES:

Chapter 21
Selfishness is not the Answer

This led to another downward spiral, fast, for me. I jumped off the wagon head first and headstrong. All commitments were off. I felt sorry for myself and I doubted God's Word. The tempter was ready to take advantage of me. A door had opened and I ran through it. Wrong door; this led straight back to alcohol.

I wrecked our marriage and so many other relationships once I started drinking again. As soon as my parole term ended, I had no one to report to and got into a band that played the bars. Guitar and singing were talents I took advantage of then. At the time I was only twenty-seven and my inhibitions were minimal. Lack of morale, respect, appreciation, commitment, and love had brought us here. I had hurt those that loved me the most because of my own selfishness and self-pity. I was getting drunk and using drugs that fed my anger towards God and committing adultery.

Once my wife and I had concurred our relationship had drawn to an end, we separated and filed for divorce. I moved in with a friend and eventually got my own place. Again, I commenced in drinking. I threw parties like I did when I was sixteen, with no cares in the world.

This all made me forget that I had been somewhere that the Lord saved me from. The booze and women were so enticing.

Then I started to date this gorgeous sweetheart, Dawn, who had been through a bad marriage and divorce. She had three kids and was providing for herself and her two girls. Her oldest had moved out already and was married. We really had an attraction, but she gave me an ultimatum on my drinking. It turned her off. She said she did not want to be with a drinker and if I wanted to drink and have multiple girlfriends, she had more self- respect than that. So I told her I wasn't answering to anyone and made my decision to keep on partying.

Not even a month later, I was arrested, again for drunk driving. They threatened to send me back to prison and I would lose everything because of my addiction to alcohol and adultery. By the grace of God, they sentenced me to tether, probation, and counseling again.

NOTES:

_____

_____

_____

_____

_____

_____

_____

_____

_____

_____

_____

_____

_____

_____

_____

_____

_____

_____

Chapter 22

God Doesn't Give Up

The counselor I had been assigned to, Chuck, was very experienced and knowledgeable. He was also the first therapist that had the motivation to discuss Christianity. At the same time, Dawn visited me. She knew of my arrest and asked, "Are you ready to quit drinking now?" She is so beautiful inside and out. Her love for the Lord puts God first in everything. He was moving in my life again to carry out His plans. God just does not give up on us. He had sent an earthly angel into my life, even though I did not deserve it; much like Christ who died for all of us, including the ones that drove nails the size of railroad spikes through His hands. We just don't deserve it, but He loves us all, His children, that much.

Dawn and I got married, and I wasn't screwing this up. I have always loved the tone of her voice and the softness that came with it, as it was so calming to me.

Proverbs 31:10-11 ~ *Who can find a virtuous wife? For her worth is far above rubies.* **11** *The heart of her husband safely trusts her; So he will have no lack of gain.*

NOTES:

_____

_____

_____

_____

_____

_____

_____

_____

_____

_____

_____

_____

_____

_____

_____

_____

_____

_____

_____

_____

Chapter 23

The Scripture will Set You Free

However, my addictive behaviours led me to smoking pot. I wanted a buzz and Dawn wasn't a smoker, but at least I managed self-control under the influence of weed. No secrets and just smoking after work when all of my daily obligations were fulfilled. This went on for a few years. Unfortunately, there was a part of me that felt convicted though. My wife was ok with it, but God wasn't.

There was still some weight on my heart from my sinful nature and pain I had caused for so many. My ex-wife and I held bitterness towards one another. The relationship with my daughter was not what I wish it could be. Still, I had been blessed. I didn't understand fully why I could feel convicted and blessed at the same time. Negative feelings are resistance to the relationship with Him.

While I have seldom been one to watch clocks, I started to notice checking the time coincidentally around 10:52. It would be either morning or evening. Then on a license plate, as I was stopped behind a car at a red light, the numerical portion was 1052. I mentioned this to my cousin and he said, "Man cuz, play that four digit three ways!" So I played it for a short period and kind of gave up. Then one day I was checking out at the same gas station I'd played the lottery at and when the cashier asked if I was playing my numbers, I declined. She then said, "Alright, your total is $10.52." What the…?

I got out to the car and told Dawn. She said, "Something is happening and you should look further into this."

The therapist that had helped me through my last drunken chapter had kept in touch by sending me a daily Bible verse. So I told Chuck what I was experiencing and he quickly responded with, "You need to read Mark 10:52." He didn't type it out, so I needed to read it myself. This Scripture was the one that would take my breath away. The Lord was reaching out to me, and it brought me to tears.

Mark 10:52 ~ *These are the words of Jesus giving sight to a blind man.* **"Your faith has made you well, now go!"**

In that moment I felt a divine peace. A veil had been removed from my eyes and weight had been lifted from my heart, as a reward to my obedience in listening to those God was working through to get to me. All the times He had sent messages and warnings, experiences of visitation (good and bad), were flashing before me. I looked up, as I knew He had removed the guilt from my heart. He had set me free! I asked Him, "Are you serious right now? You're just forgiving me like that?" I immediately felt His reassurance that He had in fact done so! *"Now go!"* I thought, *Go where God?*

Go tell it on a mountain.

The Lord works with us in specific steps; His perfect order. Our human minds do not process everything at once and He knows us better than we know ourselves. If He put everything in order in an instant, as we impatiently always want things, it would be too overwhelming, much like the face of God. In order to see Him, it would also require the ability to see *EVERYTHING* He sees. Our human state could not withstand it. Trust in His order and wait.

NOTES:

_____

_____

_____

_____

_____

_____

_____

_____

_____

_____

_____

_____

_____

_____

_____

_____

_____

_____

_____

_____

Chapter 24

The Calling

One of our daughters had gotten married and they have three boys, with one more on the way as I write. They moved to Florida for employment opportunities with our son-in-law. I also was seeking greater employment opportunities, so I decided to give up the reefer to pass any drug screening. A trip to Florida could be a chance to kick it, since I didn't know anyone down there and definitely was not about to take any pot on the plane. That's a federal offense.

We spent a week down there and I had absolutely no urges. Even though we passed some dudes fishing on the pier one day, and I noticed a fella with a blunt the size of your arm tucked behind his ear. Bob Marley types just want to smoke with everyone, but I didn't go there. Commitment is something I'm taking seriously today. The last night we were there, one of my grandsons was sitting on my lap. We were watching a movie and, all of a sudden, this great feeling of love washed over me. I was receiving a message that I am quitting everything of substance for greater reasons than just better employment.

After a week, Dawn and I got home and relished the wonderful time we had. It was then that the withdrawals set in, big time. For two weeks, I could not sleep. Now, I had quit smoking pot before like it was a breeze. This was crazy. After two weeks, the night sweats kicked in. I even had to put a towel down on the bed at night. Talk about fighting an urge. It would have been so simple to just make a call and pack a bowl. I persevered and after two weeks of that, I woke up one morning and said, "I'm going to be a pastor." Where these words had come from I didn't know at the moment, as if the Lord put the words on my tongue. Dawn said, "I know." She had visions before all of this. As a matter of fact, she shared a dream she had about our relationship; another one that gave her vision of me up on a stage with praying hands coming through the clouds. It was all coming together, God's plans.

NOTES:

Chapter 25

I Surrendered

Dawn and I had gone to church on occasion. The church we were married in was truly one that made us feel how powerful worship is. God makes His presence known when we praised and worshipped Him with all our hearts.

Mark 12:30 ~ *And you shall love the Lord your God with all your heart, with all your soul, with all your mind, and with all your strength. This is the first commandment.*

My new commitment to God was changing every process. I developed this trust that stopped worrying. My appreciation and love for Dawn and all of our family grew even stronger. People started making remarks about my "energy" everywhere I went.

At the time, I was a manager at one of our local meat markets. Thank you Jack's Market for always making room for me with the best you could offer. It was a pretty good job and the people I engaged with made it even more enjoyable. Then I ran into a guy that I had known for years. He owns five gas stations and convenience stores. He seemed excited to see me. "Mike! I am opening a market in St. Louis and you are the perfect man I need to manage it!" We got together at the market he was opening and he made me an offer I absolutely could not turn down, with hours that would allow me to attend church every Sunday and a wage that made it all the more desirable. I thought this must be some divine favour. And it was. I accepted the offer and gave my notice to my current employer at the time. He was happy for me and selected a replacement for my position.

Ready to start this new job, I was invited to have coffee with the owner of the market I planned on managing. He said, "I want you to be the owner and I will stand as silent partner." This was not what we agreed upon. I had owned a music studio on and off for nearly twenty years. The taxes I ended up owing were ridiculous; It was also an eight-day-a-week responsibility. This guy was in a predicament that had now put me in unemployment status voluntarily.

Ten years prior to this, I would have made a mess of this guy in front of all the other patrons around us and not cared about anyone else's feelings. But this new relationship I had built with Jesus kept me still. Sure, my adrenaline was flowing. I was able to manage not even cursing. I grabbed my coffee and said, "Thank you for the offer but I am not interested." I walked out the door, prayed, and went directly back to the market I had just trained my replacement at. The only position they could offer me was part time and just above minimum wage. "Alright God, what you got me doing now?"

NOTES:

_____

_____

_____

_____

_____

_____

_____

_____

_____

_____

_____

_____

_____

_____

_____

_____

_____

_____

_____

_____

Chapter 26
Funny How God Works

As soon as I was able to tell Dawn what had happened, she told me not to get upset. Trust in Him. She was so calm and understanding, like Jesus has taught us then and now.

While I immediately updated my resume, I was moved into a real study; the studying of God's Word like never before. Doctrine and stories flooded back from Catechism and Sunday school. I bought two Bibles, not just one. He was making time for me to make time for Him. So I needed more than one translation. I was going to teach people the truth and have experience to back it all up.

I was having such a hard time finding employment because of my background. A 1991 offense was haunting me. I continued to study and pray. Our church family at Holy Communion Gospel Center in Saginaw prayed with us too.

Then came a job offer that would offer opportunities and steady income. I prayed when I applied for this job and so did Dawn. My cousins wrote a letter to the president of the company. They had gone to school with him. Thank you, Glastender. I was given an opportunity to work for a company whose founding family are Christians. The company did not begin as large as it is today. In fact, it was the prayer and faith of one man that would lead to its fifty-year celebration at the time I was welcomed aboard. The Lord answers prayers in abundance. At this time, they were expanding and employing more than one hundred and fifty people.

I am not so special that I have been treated any different by God. He loves all of His children equally. Ofcourse we all have our unique experiences, but we all need each other. It's part of His divine design. He gives so much specific instruction to love Him, your neighbor, and pray even for your foes. Forgive and let God be the judge.

My life truly came into a better order once I surrendered to Him. Putting Him first brought everything else into order and a new perspective opened up for me. The veil had been lifted from my eyes, and I didn't worry or was concerned anymore about so many worldly things. I trust in Him and pray about everything.

Philippians 4:6 ~ *Be anxious for nothing, but in everything by prayer and supplication, with thanksgiving, let your requests be made known to God; and the peace of God, which surpasses all understanding, will guard your hearts and minds through Christ Jesus.*

Dawn, Dad, and I have started a ministry called The New Jerusalem. My dad and I have not only reconciled but he is my elder. He knows God's Word extremely well. He lives by it and has led me by it. We are only in the beginning of the ministry, but we owe it all to Jesus Christ to lead people away from darkness and comfort one another with the truth. After all, He laid His life down for our sake.

So I got ordained and then was baptized by one of my lifelong friends' dad has been a pastor longer than I have been alive. I know that they also prayed for me often while I was in prison. Pastor Jim Rathbun, a true man of God, baptized me before a large congregation in the presence of the Holy Spirit.

Potter's House Family Worship Center, Mt. Pleasant, Michigan 2018

NOTES:

_____

_____

_____

_____

_____

_____

_____

_____

_____

_____

_____

_____

_____

_____

_____

_____

_____

_____

Chapter 27

The Season

Our ministry is currently mobile. The Lord has us visiting with several churches to learn from them and also share with them. We did have a building for a short period; however, it was off the beaten path and could not develop a congregation large enough to cover expenses. This laid heavy on my heart for a moment. After I prayed about it, I was given an answer that this was not the season for us to be in one location.

We were given a number of confirmations that ministry is what God wants us doing. You see, God uses us to work in lives of others while He may not be seen directly with our eyes. One morning, I had just finished reading the story of the adulteress that was about to be stoned to death (**John 8:1-12**). My Bible was still open and I placed it on the coffee table in front of me. The moment I set it down, one of our members walked in the door and, with a bright, joyous smile, said, "I have something for you." As she extended her hand and opened it, there was a stone. On it was painted the words, "Faith - Hope - Love." My dad and one of our other members were seated next to me. Our mouths were open, yet we were speechless. With tears in my eyes, I asked her if she had any idea what story I had just read; she didn't have a clue. This particular stone was confirmation to us that we were on the right page and that Jesus truly is in our midst when we gather in His name.

Matthew 18:20 ~ *For where two or three are gathered in My name, I am there in the midst of them.*

A Prayer of Thanksgiving - Heavenly Father, we give You thanks for this stone that stands as confirmation. You have forgiven us and we shall forgive those who have sinned before us and against us. In Jesus's name, Amen.

NOTES:

_____

_____

_____

_____

_____

_____

_____

_____

_____

_____

_____

_____

_____

_____

_____

_____

_____

_____

Chapter 28

The Assignment

We were visiting a church one Sunday and the pastor delivering the message for the day was also a visitor. He called a number of people up to the altar to pray over them. The Holy Spirit was ever present when the pastor called me out. He said, "Pastor, I don't know why you and your wife are still in your pew. I have a message for you also." Dawn and I obediently walked up and the instant we reached the steps, he said, "Write the book." This man did not know me from Adam, and especially didn't know the fact that I'd been in the process of writing a testimonial. Up to that moment, I have to admit that I was procrastinating its completion. Tears of joy came to my eyes and I felt that spiritual love radiating around us. This lit a fire in me. Several people have asked me about writing a book. I know the Lord has spoken through them to motivate me, as my story will encourage many to seek God. He is always there. We are the ones that make it complicated.

NOTES:

_____

_____

_____

_____

_____

_____

_____

_____

_____

_____

_____

_____

_____

_____

_____

_____

_____

_____

_____

Chapter 29

Stand on the Word

In summary, the problem is our resistance against a relationship with God. Sometimes that resistance is vanity. It's so difficult to admit there is something greater than ourselves. People struggle with it because it almost always requires change or giving something up. We dismiss His efforts to connect with us in logical explanations, but the answer is faith. Let it surpass logic. Put faith into practice as though we want to get better at something. If you want to learn how to play guitar or piano, you practice. If I want to become a great artist, I will paint often.

The more we practice in our faith, through prayer and supplication, the stronger faith becomes and our relationship with God grows. Be careful not to blame the devil, because he loves taking the credit. Let us accept our responsibilities. I believe we should remember to read the Bible and gather in the name of Jesus. It truly gives us sound instruction.

NOTES:

Chapter 30

Let This Be Your Season

While I have accepted my calling from God to write this book, I hope the book will encourage its readers to write theirs! You have a testimony that may save a life or even a soul. The season for planting is now.

I also pray that many will be moved to develop their relationship with God. You can even declare your salvation right now, wherever you are in this very moment. Ask Jesus into your heart and defeat the enemy who tempts us and distracts us. Cast no stones at anyone, but cast your fears into the fire and may God work a miracle in your life right now.

Matthew 17:20 *"If someone can have faith as much as the size of a mustard seed, they can move a mountain."*

Amen

NOTES:

_____

_____

_____

_____

_____

_____

_____

_____

_____

_____

_____

_____

_____

_____

_____

_____

_____

_____

_____

Giving Thanks

I must first give thanks to the Lord. He has given me armor to adorn, and His will granted me the pardon to be set free from prison and all bondage. Let this book bring confidence into the hearts of those in need. I also give thanks to my wife, my dad, my mom, and my stepdad for their obedience to our Heavenly Father. God knows we cannot do it all on our own in this world. Thank you to all my family and friends that have supported me and encouraged me. Our prayers are being answered. To God be the Glory!

Pastor Michael B. Beeckman 2019